P9-CLE-283

JUNIATA COLLEGE LIBRARY

JUNIATA COLLEGE LIBRARY

Investigating
Ice and Glaciers

Miriam Coleman

PowerKiDS
press.

New York

Published in 2016 by The Rosen Publishing Group, Inc.
29 East 21st Street, New York, NY 10010

Copyright © 2016 by The Rosen Publishing Group, Inc.

All rights reserved. No part of this book may be reproduced in any form without permission in writing from the publisher, except by a reviewer.

First Edition

Editor: Sarah Machajewski
Book Design: Katelyn Heinle

Photo Credits: Cover kavram/Shutterstock.com; p. 4 Duncan Payne/Shutterstock.com; p. 5 Joshua Raif/Shutterstock.com; p. 7 Wildnerdpix/Shutterstock.com; pp. 8, 9 Ruth Peterkin/Shutterstock.com; p. 10 http://commons.wikimedia.org/wiki/File:Taku_glacier_firn_ice_sampling.png; p. 11 W.E. Garrett/National Geographic/Getty Images; p. 12 Wayne Scherr/Science Source/Getty Images; p. 13 (crevasse) Dimos/Shutterstock.com; p. 13 (ice cave) Peter Adams/Taxi/Getty Images; p. 14 Hyde John/Perspectives/Getty Images; p. 15 Alan Majchrowicz/Photolibrary/Getty Images; p. 17 (ice sheet) aliengrove/Jon Bowles/Moment/Getty Images; p. 17 (iceberg) Sergey Shlyaev/Shutterstock.com; p. 18 (arête) Alpine Light & Structure/Moment Open/Getty Images; p. 18 (cirque) Matt Ragen/Shutterstock.com; p. 19 S.R.Lee Photo Traveller/Shutterstock.com; p. 21 Gardawind/Shutterstock.com; p. 22 Ignacio Palacios/Lonely Planet Images/Getty Images.

Coleman, Miriam.
 Investigating ice and glaciers / Miriam Coleman.
    pages cm. — (Earth science detectives)
 Includes bibliographical references and index.
 ISBN 978-1-4777-5947-9 (pbk.)
 ISBN 978-1-4777-5948-6 (6 pack)
 ISBN 978-1-4777-5946-2 (library binding)
 1. Glaciers—Juvenile literature. I. Title.
 GB2403.8.C65 2015
 551.31'2—dc23
                                    2014031157

Manufactured in the United States of America

CPSIA Compliance Information: Batch #WS15PK: For Further Information contact Rosen Publishing, New York, New York at 1-800-237-9932

CONTENTS

CURR
GB
240.38
.C65
2015

MYSTERIES IN THE ICE

Have you ever looked at a tall mountain or low valley and wondered where it came from? It didn't just appear out of nowhere. Many of Earth's **landscapes** were formed by glaciers. Glaciers are giant masses of ice that have shaped mountains, canyons, rivers, and valleys. They've been shaping Earth for hundreds of thousands of years.

Although these giant forces have come and gone from many areas, they've left behind clues we can use to discover what happened long ago. In areas where glaciers still exist, we can see how they're still shaping Earth today.

Glacial ice carved out this valley long ago.

What clues do ice and glaciers contain about Earth's landscapes and changing **climate**? Let's find out!

WHAT IS A GLACIER?

Glaciers are giant, slow-moving **formations** of ice. The ice was once snow that remained in a place without melting. Over time, **layers** of snow built up and became packed tightly together to form glaciers.

Glaciers can be hundreds of miles long or as small as a football field. They can grow to be several miles thick. They can be thousands or even millions of years old.

Today, glaciers cover about 10 percent of Earth's land, although they once covered much more, including parts of oceans.

CLUE ME IN

The Lambert-Fisher Glacier in Antarctica is the biggest glacier in the world. It's 250 miles (400 km) long and up to 60 miles (100 km) wide!

Scientists often think of glaciers as great rivers of ice. They flow like water does, only much more slowly.

WHERE ARE GLACIERS?

Glaciers form in areas that receive plenty of snowfall in winter and are cool enough in summer so that snow doesn't melt. Glaciers used to cover about one-third of the planet. Today, they're mostly found at the North and the South Poles and in high mountain areas.

Most of the world's glacier ice (about 91 percent) is in Antarctica. Greenland has the second-highest amount of glaciers. In the United States, glaciers are found in the mountain ranges of many western states and in Alaska. The Himalayas in Asia, Mount Kilimanjaro in Africa, and the Alps in Europe also have glacier formations.

Glacier Bay National Park in Alaska has 16 glaciers. People can visit the park to see the glaciers, but there are also areas for hiking, camping, fishing, bird watching, and more.

CLUE ME IN

Glaciers contain more than just clues about Earth's land and climate. They also contain 75 percent of the world's freshwater supply—but it's frozen!

MAKING ICY GIANTS

Glaciers begin with snowfall. Snow must fall for a long time in places where it's too cold to melt. The snow piles up in layers. The weight of the new snow **compresses** snow below it. This **pressure** causes the snow crystals to re-form into ice crystals.

Over time, the ice crystals become larger. The air between the crystals is forced out, and the ice becomes very thick and heavy. As more snow falls and adds more weight, the ice builds up and turns into a glacier. This process can take more than a hundred years.

CLUE ME IN
"Firn" is the name for the half-snow, half-ice mixture that gets compressed into glacier ice.

Scientists can study a glacier's layers to understand the differences between snow crystals and ice crystals and how they come together to make glaciers.

PARTS OF A GLACIER

Scientists learn a lot by studying the parts of a glacier. The accumulation area is the part of the glacier where snow falls and adds to the glacier's size. It's usually the glacier's highest part.

Sometimes there are giant cracks in a glacier, called crevasses. They're a sign that parts of a glacier are moving at different speeds or that a glacier is sliding over ice that doesn't belong to it. Some glaciers have ice caves. They're proof that water has traveled either through or under a glacier. Ice caves often **collapse** as glaciers melt.

moraine

CLUE ME IN

Glaciers pick up rocks and soil as they move and drop them as they melt. The matter left behind is called a moraine. Moraines only appear in areas that have or once had ice in them.

ice cave

crevasse

Moraines, crevasses, and ice caves are just some clues scientists can study to learn about the activity that happens in and around glaciers.

KINDS OF GLACIERS

There are many kinds of glaciers. The largest type is called a continental ice sheet. This type is found only in Greenland and Antarctica. Ice sheets are very important. They play a big role in forming and **maintaining** the earth's climate.

Ice caps are like ice sheets, but smaller. They're found mostly in flat, high areas near the poles. Ice fields are areas of connected ice caps and glaciers. Ice fields are shaped by the land underneath them. Mountain glaciers form in high mountain areas. Valley glaciers flow down into valleys from mountain glaciers. They look like giant tongues!

CLUE ME IN

A tidewater glacier is a glacier that flows far enough to reach the sea. Large pieces of ice that break off from these glaciers are called icebergs.

iceberg

This image shows a glacier branching off from an ice sheet.

SLOWLY SHAPING EARTH

Glaciers are important because they've shaped much of Earth's **terrain**. The heavy weight of glacial ice erodes, or wears away, the surface of the land it moves over. This force can carve deep valleys into mountains.

As glaciers cut away at mountains, they can leave cirques, which are bowl-shaped hollows in a mountainside. They also make narrow ridges called arêtes, as well as horns, which are pointed peaks.

cirque

arête

Glaciers leave their mark long after they've left an area. When glaciers retreat, they often leave behind ridges or mounds of rock and soil. They also leave behind lakes whose water came from melted ice.

horn

Glaciers created these kinds of formations thousands of years ago. Without glaciers, we wouldn't have such beautiful landscapes to enjoy.

READING CLUES

During the last **ice age**, glaciers covered about 32 percent of Earth's land. As the climate warms and more snow melts than falls, glaciers shrink. In the last hundred years, some glaciers have even disappeared.

Glacial ice holds clues that can teach us how the climate has changed over time. Sometimes scientists drill deep into the core of a glacier and study air bubbles trapped in the ice. They find out what was in the air around Earth when the ice formed. They also look to see if there are any gases in the glaciers that would affect the climate if they were released. The results show how Earth has changed, or could change, over time.

Melting glaciers, such as the one shown here, cause sea levels to rise. This could affect farming, the amount of water available for people and animals, and many kinds of ecosystems.

THE PAST AND PRESENT

Glaciers have been shaping Earth for millions of years—from ancient ice ages to the present day. Formed from tiny snowflakes, these giant masses of moving ice have left their mark all over the globe.

As glaciers grow and move across the land, they gather and freeze clues about Earth's history. As they retreat, they **reveal** clues for scientists to study. If we learn how to read the clues, we can discover a great deal about Earth's past as well as changes happening today.

GLOSSARY

climate: The average weather conditions of a place over a period of time.

collapse: To cave in.

compress: To press or squeeze together.

ecosystem: A community of living things.

formation: A structure or arrangement of something.

ice age: A period of time in which much of Earth's surface is covered in ice.

indicator: Something that shows the state of something else.

landscape: The visible features of an area of land.

layer: One thickness lying over or under another.

maintain: To keep something the same.

pressure: The force that pushes on something else.

reveal: To show.

temperature: How hot or cold something is.

terrain: The features of an area of land.

INDEX

WEBSITES

Due to the changing nature of Internet links, PowerKids Press has developed an online list of websites related to the subject of this book. This site is updated regularly. Please use this link to access the list: www.powerkidslinks.com/det/glac